ULTIMATE FIGHTING

THE BRAINS AND BRAWN OF MIXED MARTIAL ARTS

PATRICK JONES

MILLBROOK PRESS · MINNEAPOLIS

NOTE TO READERS: This book provides general information about the sport of mixed martial arts. It is not intended to serve as a how-to guide. Anyone who engages in mixed martial arts does so at his or her own risk and should only do so under the supervision of a trained coach or other instructor.

Millbrook Press
A division of Lerner Publishing Group, Inc.
241 First Avenue North
Minneapolis, MN 55401 U.S.A.

Website address: www.lernerbooks.com

Library of Congress Cataloging-in-Publication Data

Jones, Patrick, 1961–
    Ultimate fighting : the brains and brawn of mixed martial arts / by Patrick Jones.
      pages   cm. — (Spectacular sports)
    Includes index.
    ISBN 978–1–4677–0934–7 (lib. bdg. : alk. paper)
    ISBN 978–1–4677–1711–3 (eBook)
    1. Mixed martial arts—Juvenile literature. I. Title.
GV1102.7.M59J66 2014
796.8—dc23
                                         2012048932

Manufactured in the United States of America
1 – PC – 7/15/13

CONTENTS

Fans pack the arena to watch the Ultimate
Fighting Championship 112 event in the
United Arab Emirates in April 2010.

INTRODUCTION:
WHAT IF?

What if? What if a boxer and a wrestler stepped into the ring together? Who would win? What if a fighter skilled in the martial art of Brazilian jiu-jitsu (BJJ) tangled with an equally skilled foe in traditional judo? Who would come out on top?

People asked questions such as these for decades. Imagine a no-holds-barred bout between boxing legend Muhammad Ali and martial arts master Bruce Lee. It would have been an amazing clash of styles. But at the time, it was just a fantasy. The sport of mixed martial arts (MMA) didn't exist when these athletes were in their prime.

That changed beginning in the 1980s. The new sport of MMA allowed fighters with very different skill sets to square off. The sport allowed fans to answer that question—*what if?* And soon an entirely new style, suited just for the Octagon cage of MMA, would emerge.

Over the past three decades, MMA has grown from a violent, no-holds-barred sport into an international sensation. Want to learn more about one of the fastest-growing sports in the world? Turn the page. In the words of legendary MMA referee Big John McCarthy: "Are you ready? Are you ready? Let's get it on!"

Two young men are shown wrestling on this stone relief from 510 B.C. in Athens, Greece.

BATTLEGROUNDS:
FROM ANCIENT GREECE TO THE OCTAGON

Combat sports are nothing new. The term *martial arts* wasn't coined until the 1500s, but the history of combat sports stretches back thousands of years. The ancient Greeks made wrestling an Olympic sport in 708 B.C. Soon after, an early form of boxing joined it in the Olympic Games.

As the Greeks watched wrestlers and boxers, they must have wondered who would win a match between the two.

PANKRATION: SUDDEN DEATH

The 33rd Olympics in 684 B.C. introduced pankration. This "all strength" contest featured two combatants in a nearly no-holds-barred match. Only eye gouging and biting were outlawed. Men could punch and kick. Once on the ground, they could use submission holds to attempt to get their opponents to give up the fight.

Some fights dragged on and on. If a fight lasted until sunset, it required the *klimax*. The fighters drew lots (kind of like a coin flip) to see who went first. The first fighter delivered a strike. His foe was not allowed to block. If that strike didn't end the fight, then the second fighter got his turn. Very few turns were needed before the fight—and sometimes a life—ended.

Pankration changed over time. It evolved into two types: stand-up fighting *(ano)* and ground fighting *(kato)*. In A.D. 404, the Romans, who had taken over Greece, shut down the Olympics and official pankration contests ceased. The sport, however, did not die. In Europe a variation called *brancaille* developed. It was based on wrestling but allowed competitors to use their hands, feet, elbows, and knees to strike their opponents.

Meanwhile, martial arts flourished around the world. Different cultures developed distinct forms of fighting. Among them were sambo in Russia, ju-jitsu in Japan, muay Thai in Thailand, and tae kwan do in Korea.

SHOW BUSINESS

Combat sports grew popular in the United States in the 1800s. A form of wrestling with few rules, called catch wrestling, had become popular. The rough-and-tumble sport of boxing was as dangerous as it was exciting.

Over time, more rules governed the sport of boxing, making it safer for combatants. Meanwhile, wrestling was undergoing another type of change. In the 1800s and the early 1900s, most wrestling matches were shoots. This meant that the matches were real, with no fixed outcomes. But at some point in the early 1900s, the sport became more about show business. Wrestling featured colorful characters and worked (predetermined) outcomes. It was no longer a real combat sport. Both boxing and wrestling remained popular. They thrived with the dawn of television in the 1950s.

After World War II (1939–1945), martial arts, particularly karate, became popular in the United States. Dojos (martial arts schools) sprang up all over. An American form called kempo, or full-contact karate, developed. Movies introduced many people to martial arts, mostly because of one man—Bruce Lee.

ENTER THE DRAGON: BRUCE LEE AND JEET KUNE DO

As a teenager in Hong Kong, Bruce Lee got into street fights. His parents made him channel that energy into the martial arts. He soon became a master. In 1959 Lee moved to the United States and opened his first dojo, in Seattle, Washington. Soon after, a TV producer saw him at a karate tournament in California. The producer cast Lee for *The Green Hornet* TV show, which ran from 1966 to 1967. The show wasn't a hit, but Bruce Lee was!

Lee wanted to star in movies. But he couldn't land any lead roles in Hollywood. So he returned to Hong Kong to make kung fu movies. Films such as *Way of the Dragon* shattered box office records in Asia and made big money in the

Bruce Lee delivers a head kick in a scene from *Enter the Dragon* in 1973. *Enter the Dragon* was the final film Lee made before his death in July 1973.

United States. In *Way of the Dragon,* the final fight scene featured Lee and Chuck Norris, another martial artist who went on to become an action star.

Lee died in 1973. But he had already helped to make martial arts popular worldwide. Perhaps less known, yet even more important to the development of MMA, was Lee's fight philosophy. Even while working in films, Lee often sparred with other martial arts experts. He found that traditional martial arts were too much science, with their strict rules, and too little art. Also, while martial arts looked dangerous, in a real fight, many such moves would fail. Lee came up with the idea of jeet kune do, or "way of intercepting the fist." This was a hybrid style. It combined the style of martial arts with real-world effectiveness. Jeet kune do emphasized practicality, flexibility, speed, and efficiency. Fighters cross-trained in all combat arts, including boxing and even fencing. In many ways, Lee developed ideas to create the first true mixed martial artists. That is, if you don't ask the Gracie family in Brazil.

THE GRACIE CHALLENGE

Meanwhile, another version of mixed martial arts was emerging in Brazil. Its roots went back to the early 1900s. Mitsuyo Maeda was a Japanese judo expert and pro wrestler at that time. He challenged anyone in the crowd to fight him, and he beat them all. His nickname was King of Combat. Maeda settled in Brazil and performed judo exhibits to promote his dojo. These shows showed how a smaller man (Maeda weighed only 140 pounds [64 kilograms]) could defeat a larger man using skill and leverage. Fourteen-year-old Carlos Gracie saw one of the shows in 1917. He soon joined Maeda's dojo in the northern state of Para, Brazil.

Four years later, Gracie moved to Rio de Janeiro, Brazil. There, he opened his own dojo with his younger brother Helio. The brothers were very different. Carlos was large and strong. Helio was small. He couldn't match his brother's strength. So he created a fighting system for those who weren't powerful enough to execute the throws crucial to success in judo. He called it Gracie jiu-jitsu, but it would later be dubbed Brazilian jiu-jitsu. This martial art still used judo throws. But they existed mainly for the purpose of getting an opponent to the ground, where a combatant would attempt to win with choke holds and joint holds. Confident with his new system, Helio issued challenges to all kinds of fighters to an anything-goes fight called *vale tudo*.

In 1995 Helio Gracie held up an old newspaper article about his jiu-jitsu fighting style.

In 1951 four-time Japan judo champion Masahiko Kimura accepted the challenge. In front of 20,000 people, he battled Gracie in perhaps the first large public MMA battle. Kimura got Gracie in a judo hold called *ude-garami* (later called the Kimura). The hold broke Gracie's arm, but the tough Brazilian refused to give up! His brother Carlos threw a towel into the ring to signal Gracie's surrender.

Stunned by the loss, Helio retired. He focused on spreading the word of BJJ and raising his family. One son, Rorion, brought BJJ to the United States in 1978. Like Bruce Lee, Rorion ended up in the movies. His dojo became popular among Hollywood stars. His fame spread when he revived the Gracie challenge by inviting fighters from all martial arts to battle him. Many challenged Rorion, but all lost. BJJ seemed to be the ultimate fighting style.

In Brazil, Helio came out of retirement to battle former student Waldemar Santana. Helio hated that Santana had become a pro wrestler. A war of words in the press led to a fight, not in public but at a local gym. The two men fought for four hours! Gracie finally succumbed when Santana kicked him in the head.

KICK-STARTING MMA

Another kick to the head was even more important in MMA history. It came from the foot of Akira Maeda. A trained karate fighter, Maeda was a protégé of the New Japan pro wrestling promotion's biggest star Antonio Inoki. Maeda became an excellent pro wrestler. But he didn't like the emphasis on entertainment. He left New Japan to start his own promotion, the Universal Wrestling Federation (UWF). Three other wrestlers—Satoru Sayama, Nobuhiko Takada, and Yoshiaki Fujiwara—joined him.

The four promoted shoot-style wrestling. It featured hard kicks, submission holds, and judo throws but no leaps from the top rope. The fights were still worked, but they *looked* real. The UWF did well at first, but infighting led to its demise. Three of the four returned to New Japan. In 1985 Sayama started a new promotion called Shooto. It featured no pulled punches and few holds barred. It was the first true MMA group.

INOKI VS. ALI

Antonio Inoki's New Japan Wrestling was struggling for survival in the mid-1970s. Inoki was determined to prove that he was the nation's best wrestler. He challenged and defeated karate masters, judo experts, and other martial arts experts from all over the world. Next, he set his sights on boxing heavyweight champion Muhammad Ali.

Inoki offered Ali millions of dollars to come to Japan for the match. Ali agreed to take part in—and lose—a worked fight. But the champ later changed his mind. He refused to lose. Thus, the first real mixed martial arts match occurred on June 26, 1976 *(below)*. For 15 rounds, Inoki kicked at Ali's legs, while Ali threw punches that missed. Fittingly, the fight ended in a draw, as there were no winners that night. It may have been the first ultimate fight, but it was ultimately boring!

Maeda returned to New Japan to deliver the kick that would help launch MMA. During a match in 1987, he did the unthinkable. He threw a real kick to the face of former Olympic wrestler Riki Choshu. The kick broke a bone in Choshu's face. It was Maeda's farewell in New Japan. He quit the company instead of being fired or facing harsh punishment. By 1988 he'd restarted the UWF. This time, his promotion caught on. Fans believed that UWF fights were real. They weren't real, but fans loved it.

The first UWF show sold out in 15 minutes. Within a year, Maeda headlined a match in the Tokyo Dome before 50,000 fans. Yet once again, disagreement over the direction of the company led to a crash. Takada started a new promotion called Union of Wrestling Forces International (UWFI). It featured pro and amateur wrestling stars battling in worked matches promoted as real fights.

Meanwhile, Fujiwara formed a promotion called Pancrase. It featured a variation of pankration. One of its early stars was American Ken Shamrock. With his muscular physique and tough-guy look, Shamrock became the first MMA star. He was touted as the world's most dangerous man.

THE OCTAGON

By the 1990s, the worldwide popularity of boxing was declining. Wrestling no longer even resembled real fighting. Meanwhile, action movies starring martial artists such as Chuck Norris and Jean-Claude Van Damme were hot. Among them was Van Damme's *Bloodsport* (1988). It centered on a character fighting in an illegal full-contact martial arts tournament—in other words, ultimate fighting.

In California the Gracie challenge had caught the attention of the press, as well as that of businessman Art Davie. Davie teamed

Jean-Claude Van Damme *(center)* in a scene from the movie *Bloodsport* (1988)

with Gracie to produce a series of videos *(Gracies in Action)* and formed a company called War of the Worlds (WOW). The company promised to deliver real fighting action. But TV networks declined to air it. Gracie and Davie knew where boxing and wrestling made their money: on pay-per-view (PPV). PPV allowed people to pay to watch live events in the comfort of their own homes.

While Gracie and Davie had an idea, they lacked partners. WOW reached out to a PPV company called Semaphore Entertainment Group (SEG). The groups partnered to form Ultimate Fighting Championship (UFC). One early UFC supporter was Gracie student John Milius. Milius came up with the signature symbol of the UFC: the eight-sided cage called the Octagon.

THE NUMBERING GAME

The first UFC PPV event in 1993 wasn't called UFC 1 at the time. After all, the promoters had planned for just one event! After that, UFC events were billed with catchy marketing titles, such as *As Real as It Gets* (UFC 50). It wasn't until UFC 100 in 2009 that these events were called by their numbers. Fans liked the numbering system and began applying it all the way back to UFC 1. As the sport grew, so did the number of these big events. By 2006 PPV events were happening monthly. The final event of 2012 was UFC 156.

With the tagline *there are no rules,* UFC 1 took place in Denver, Colorado, on November 12, 1993. It featured a tournament format with few rules, no weight classes, and no time limits. Rorion Gracie picked his younger brother Royce to represent the family and BJJ. In the first round, Gracie submitted boxer Patrick Smith in less than two minutes. Gracie took down Ken Shamrock with a choke hold in the second round. Gracie won the tournament by submitting karate expert Gerard Gordeau. The event proved two things: that BJJ was the best fighting system and that people would pay to see this blood sport.

DOWN BUT NOT OUT

The early UFC lived up to its billing of mixed martial arts combat with contestants for all the fighting sports. It included sumo wrestlers, kickboxers, and college wrestlers. UFC 5 marked a turning point. While it still featured the tournament format (won by Dan Severn), it also offered the first main event "Superfight," a rematch between Gracie and Shamrock. UFC also added time limits to the fights. That change was fortunate because the main event ended in a draw after a 30-minute fight with a five-minute overtime. The Gracies opposed the rule changes and left the UFC.

The sport also had other detractors. One of them was U.S. senator John McCain of Arizona. McCain objected to the violence of the MMA. He sought to force the UFC itself into submission. He almost succeeded when 36 states banned the sport!

Under political pressure, PPV companies stopped the broadcasts. The UFC was forced to adapt. It quickly made a number of rule changes. It also stressed that MMA was a sport, not just a street fight.

The rule changes involved both the structure of the bouts and the moves allowed. The new rules created weight classes and time limits. They also required fighters to wear gloves. Many moves were banned, such as head-butting, hair pulling, and kicking a downed foe in the head. The changes lead to an evolution in the MMA style. Fights

Ken Shamrock *(top)* pins Royce Gracie during their "Superfight" at UFC 5 in 1995.

remained showdowns between competing strategies. But more fighters cross-trained. Under the new rules, wrestlers such as Mark Coleman reigned supreme. Coleman used his wrestling to get his foe to mat and then began striking. This style became known as ground and pound. MMA fighting was becoming a style of its own.

The rule changes made a difference. Soon political pressure against the UFC eased. The UFC grew in the United States as well as overseas. Still, the company was losing money. In 2001 the owners sold it to Zuffa, a company belonging to casino-owning brothers Frank and Lorenzo Fertitta. Lorenzo hired his boyhood friend Dana White as president. White rebranded UFC to be a sport, not a spectacle. That helped bring back the PPV companies. As professional wrestling's popularity peaked in 2001, UFC was able to promote its product to a wider audience—wrestling fans who wanted a taste of the real thing.

UFC 30 marked the beginning of a new era. It was the first event under the new ownership. And it was headlined by a charismatic up-and-coming star named Tito Ortiz. UFC had survived, and it was stronger than ever.

THE GOLDEN AGE

Under White's leadership, UFC fought its way into the mainstream. In 2002 Fox Sports Net broadcast a middleweight title bout between Chuck Liddell and Vitor Belfort. Other stars also raised UFC's profile. Among them was Ken Shamrock, who had wrestled in World Wrestling Entertainment (WWE). He used his skills on the microphone to promote a fight with Ortiz. The two talked trash, just as pro wrestlers would, leading up to the fight, called Vendetta. The public ate it up. The fight came at UFC 40, an event that saw the PPV audience triple. Sports media outlets such as ESPN and *Sports Illustrated* had begun covering UFC fights just like any other sporting event. The public was finally viewing MMA as a legitimate sport.

Tito Ortiz *(right)* throws a punch at Ken Shamrock during UFC 40 (2002).

This began the golden age of UFC. Legends such as Ortiz, Liddell, Matt Hughes, and Randy Couture battled in front of sold-out arenas coast to coast. In January 2005, UFC created *The Ultimate Fighter* reality show, which ran on Spike TV. It featured young fighters battling for a UFC contract. The exciting slugfest finale between Forrest Griffin and Stephan Bonnar catapulted UFC to popularity.

PRIDE

As UFC grew, other MMA promotions sprang up. Many featured fighters who came from UFC. But some, such as Strikeforce, developed their own talent. Few of these new promotions lasted long. But one, the Japan-based Pride Fighting Championships, was ready to compete with UFC.

Takada started Pride in 1997. At first Pride was mostly shoot matches, though a few matches were worked to protect Takada, the promotion's biggest star. One such fight featured Takada defeating former UFC champion Mark Coleman. In Pride's first TV broadcast, Takada lost to Rickson Gracie, Rorion Gracie's brother, before a crowd of 47,000.

Soon all Pride fights were real. But the company kept the spectacle of pro wrestling. Pride fighters made grand entrances with blaring music and fireworks. Because Pride had fewer rules than UFC, longer time limits, and better pay, the best fighters in the world flocked to Japan. MMA legends such as Wanderlei Silva and Antonio Rodrigo Nogueira mixed it up with Japanese fighters in thrilling contests. Kazushi Sakuraba, a former pro wrestler, became a legend as the Gracie Hunter, defeating four members of the first family of MMA. For MMA fans, the question was no longer could a boxer defeat a wrestler, but which was better: UFC or Pride?

UFC: THE BASICS

The UFC in the early days had no time periods (rounds), standard attire, weight classes, or judging. Inside the Octagon, only eye gouging and biting were prohibited. By 2000 that had changed. The Unified Rules of Mixed Martial Arts gave MMA the structured rules that helped the sport gain mainstream acceptance. Here are some of the major rules.

- Rounds: Three rounds of five minutes each with a one-minute rest period in between rounds. Title matches can be sanctioned for five rounds.
- Attire: All competitors must fight in approved shorts and without shoes. Shirts, judo jackets, and long pants are not allowed. Fighters must use approved light gloves that allow fingers to grab. A mouth guard and a protective cup are also required.
- Weight classes: There are nine weight classes. They range from flyweight to super heavyweight.
- Judging criteria: Three judges score each round. The winner of each receives 10 points, and the loser receives nine points or fewer.
- Fouls: There are 28 fouls, including head-butting, hair-pulling, and placing a finger into any cut (gross!). Prohibited strikes include any attack to the groin, the kidneys, the spine, or the back of the head or downward elbow strikes. Kicking, kneeing, or stomping on a fighter on the ground are not allowed.

TOTAL DOMINATION

Pride's time at the top didn't last. The promotion suffered a series of scandals. Sponsors left the promotion. Many top fighters returned to UFC. In 2007 the UFC bought Pride. UFC was dominating the MMA market. The addition of one heavy hitter—Brock Lesnar—made UFC's conquest complete.

Lesnar had been a great college wrestler. He had gone on to dominate WWE. But Lesnar didn't enjoy pro wrestling. He left WWE. After a failed attempt to play pro football, he turned to MMA. The hype for his 2007 debut against former UFC heavyweight champ Frank Mir was tremendous. Lesnar lost, but a star was born.

Brock Lesnar *(right)* spars with Heath Herring during UFC 87 in 2008.

Lesnar won his next fight and then beat former champ Randy Couture. Many felt Lesnar was the true champion, since he'd been the one to beat Couture. But UFC had awarded the title to Frank Mir. That set up a rematch between Lesnar and Mir. The winner would be the undisputed champion. They met at UFC 100 in 2009. The event topped 1.6 million PPV buys and received huge mainstream coverage. Lesnar's huge popularity drew in new UFC fans. Revenue soared.

Flush with cash, Zuffa bought out Strikeforce in 2011. By doing so, it gained access to future MMA legends such as Nick Diaz, Jake Shields, and Urijah Faber. Strikeforce's main contribution to MMA long term, however, may have been its women's division. Stars such as Gina Carano and Ronda Rousey showed fans that women were just as tough and skilled as male fighters.

In just a few decades, MMA has grown from a violent spectacle into a widely popular sport. Most events on PPV draw more viewers than the biggest boxing matches or WWE events. Finally, fans no longer need to wonder *what if.*

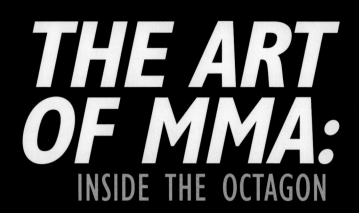

2

THE ART OF MMA:
INSIDE THE OCTAGON

Many early UFC fights resembled brawls more than athletic competitions. Fighters such as Royce Gracie and Dan Severn brought skill and tactics to the Octagon. But many others, such as Tank Abbott, brought little more than raw strength. Others, such as 700-pound (318 kg) sumo wrestler Emanuel Yarborough, were pure spectacle. Often the UFC looked more like a tough-man contest than a true sport.

When the Gracies left after UFC 5, the influence of BJJ waned. Mark Coleman and other wrestlers dominated. As the sport entered the 21st century, Bruce Lee's vision of versatile, cross-trained fighters emerged. Fighters such as Tito Ortiz and Chuck Liddell became true mixed martial artists. Yet, while the sport has evolved and the rules have changed, some things, such as strikes, submissions, and takedowns, have stayed the same.

THE RULES

Adopted in 2000, the Unified Rules of Mixed Martial Arts govern MMA contests. These rules spell out everything that is and is not allowed during a fight. The rules dictate that fights last three rounds of five minutes each, except championship fights, which are five rounds. The referee can end a fight at any time he feels a fighter is no longer able to defend himself. If the fight goes the distance, then three judges decide the winner based on a system that awards 10 points to the round winner and nine or fewer points to the round loser. According to the rules, the judges base their decision on mixed martial arts techniques, such as effective striking, effective grappling, control of the ring/fighting area, effective aggressiveness, and defense. These rules are constantly reviewed and adjusted to suit the evolving sport.

LET'S GET IT ON!

Most fights start with the fighters, as a show of respect, touching gloves in the center of the ring. Fighters circle each other looking for an opportunity to strike or attempt a takedown. In the early days of MMA, many fights ended quickly—sometimes with a single punch! But most modern MMA fighters take a more tactical approach. For example, Anderson Silva likes to carefully feel out his opponents. Of course, some fighters still prefer to mix it up right away. Dan Henderson comes out of his corner throwing bombs. These widely varying strategies help keep the sport interesting.

STRIKES

MMA features hundreds of strikes. But they all come down to four main classes: fist, foot, knee, and elbow. Fist strikes are also called punches, while strikes using the feet are kicks. But that doesn't mean that all strikes within a type are the same. For example, a fist strike can be as simple as a straight boxing jab. But it can also be as dynamic as a spinning back fist, in which the fighter spins all the way around before landing the punch.

MMA fighters employ a wide range of kicks. Some, such as head kicks, are designed to end a fight by knockout. Meanwhile, leg kicks are intended to wear down an opponent over time. Brock Lesnar's loss to former Strikeforce champ Alistair Overeem at UFC 141 was the result of a hard kick to his midsection (liver kick).

Elbow strikes are especially effective on the ground. MMA rules prohibit straight up-and-down elbow shots (called 12/6 shots, for the position of the numbers on a clockface) on a foe. But a relentless barrage of elbows across the face often results in a fight being called (ended by the referee).

Some fighters rely on knee strikes. Fighters hold tightly onto an opponent's head (called a clinch) and unleash powerful knee strikes. Anderson Silva is known for his ability to push his opponent's head down at the moment he brings his knee up. The math is simple: knee plus face equals knockout!

The best fighters employ all four strikes and from both the right and the left. Strikes can end a fight, but hard strikes may only stun a fighter and knock him to the ground to start the pounding. More often it's not a strike but a takedown that brings the fight to the mat.

Jose Aldo *(right)* lands a straight right jab to Frankie Edgar's face.

Jon Jones slams Stephan Bonnar in the face with his knee.

TAKEDOWNS

In the early UFC, pure strikers rarely stood a chance against fighters trained in wrestling or BJJ. Strikers couldn't defend themselves against takedowns such as wrestling's single-leg takedown or judo's sweeping hip throw.

The keys to every takedown are leverage, position, and timing. Some are spectacular. For example, in a suplex, a fighter lifts his foe off the ground and then uses his body weight to slam the opponent down. The force of the takedown itself can even knock a fighter out. Other takedowns, such as a hip throw, are designed simply to bring the fight to the ground. When a fighter attempts a takedown, he shoots (makes a sudden, aggressive move) on his foe. It is from this move that the pro wrestling term *shoot* came to mean any move that is real.

Takedown defenses vary, but the sprawl and brawl is most effective. The fighter sprawls by moving his body, in particular the legs, away from his foe. This position makes it hard for an opponent to achieve a takedown. The fighter attempting the takedown is on the offense and is less able to defend himself, especially against uppercuts and knees. Sometimes the shooter gets shot with a hard strike that ends the fight.

Dominick Cruz *(bottom)* takes down Demetrious Johnson with a suplex.

ON THE GROUND

Just because a fighter finds himself on his back, that doesn't mean a fight's over. In fact, a smart fighter can turn being on his back to his advantage. What made BJJ so effective was the ability of a fighter to win while on his back! The guard position from the bottom lets the downed fighter control the movement of the fighter on top. There are two main types of guard: closed and rubber. In a closed guard, the fighter on his back locks his legs around the back of the fighter on top. In a rubber guard, the fighter on his back locks one leg around his foe's neck and hooks his leg with his own hand.

Michael Johnson *(bottom)* uses a closed guard position against Myles Jury.

But it is hard to submit someone when he is punching you in the face! When a fighter employs ground and pound, he simply gets his opponent down and starts throwing strikes. The fighter on top takes a mount position, sitting on his opponent's chest. From this position, few opponents can offer much defense. A steady supply of elbows and fists can end a fight quickly.

SUBMISSION HOLDS

Most submission holds have their origins in judo. To submit a foe, a fighter must gain control of a body part—usually an arm or a leg. The fighter forces the leg or the arm into a position that causes his opponent pain. When the pain becomes too great—or the hold threatens permanent damage—the fighter submits. A fighter indicates a submission by tapping out—tapping the mat or his opponent's body.

Upper body submissions include the Kimura. This hold puts tremendous pressure on the shoulder joint as the fighter uses leverage, position, and power to control his foe's arm. Another upper body submission is the keylock. From side mount, a fighter grabs his opponent's wrist with his near hand and reaches under that arm with his free hand, grabbing his own forearm. Once applied, a fighter can use a keylock to apply unbearable pressure to his opponent's elbow.

Kenny Roberston *(left)* applies a joint lock submission to Brock Jardine's leg. The move put tremendous pressure on Jardine's hamstring, forcing him to tap out.

Lower body submissions focus on joints such as the ankle and the knees. For example, the heel hook has one fighter placing both his legs around the leg of an opponent while holding the foot attached to that leg in his armpit. Then the fighter twists the ankle while holding the heel with the forearm. Joints in the body are meant to bend one way. When they are bent the other way, it's time to tap out!

CHOKE HOLDS

Choke holds are another way of quickly ending a fight. The goal of a choke hold is simple—to give your opponent a short nap. There are two types of choke holds: blood chokes and air chokes.

For a blood choke, a fighter applies pressure to his opponent's neck. The pressure cuts off the supply of blood to the brain, which quickly leads to unconsciousness. Blood chokes often end a fight quickly. The hardest to escape is the rear naked choke. Applied from behind, the fighter wraps his arms around his opponent's neck, his forearm against one side of the neck and his bicep against the other side.

Air chokes are designed to cut off a fighter's supply of oxygen by making breathing difficult. The triangle choke is one common air choke. It uses the same idea as the rear naked choke—pressure against the neck. But the fighter uses his legs instead—and a fighter's legs are always stronger than his arms. The triangle can be applied from the

Alexander Gustafsson uses a rear naked choke against James Te Huna.

guard position and usually ends fights. One variation of the triangle is the gogoplata, where the fighter locks his foe's neck between his shin and forearm.

WINNING THE FIGHT

Once a fight begins, MMA battles can end in one of five ways.

1. Submission—a fighter taps out from being locked in a painful hold from which he can't escape.
2. Knockout (KO)—a fighter is out cold. Most knockouts come from strikes, but a choke hold can also result in a KO.
3. Technical knockout (TKO)—a fight ends because a referee determines a fighter is no longer able to defend himself. A TKO may also occur when a ringside doctor tells the referee to end the fight because of an injury or because a fighter's management concedes by "throwing in the towel."
4. Judges' decision—three judges determine the winner of a fight that goes the distance. Decisions can be unanimous (all three judges agree), split (two judges score the fight for one fighter, but the third judge scores it for his opponent), or majority (two judges score the bout for one fighter while the third scores it a draw). The rarest judges' decision is the draw, in which the judges determine that neither fighter won.
5. Disqualification (DQ)—a fighter loses the match for breaking the rules.

3 STANDING OVATIONS:
12 CLASSIC MMA FIGHTS

The first fight at UFC 1 wasn't much of a contest. Dutch karate kid Gerard Gordeau defeated American sumo wrestler Teila Tuli in less than 30 seconds. Most of the fights at that first event were similar—quick knockouts or submissions. Only one bout lasted more than four minutes. Fans were interested because of UFC's reputation for brutality. But the first fights didn't live up to the hype.

That soon changed. Modern MMA fans look for the same qualities in a fight that fans of team sports look for in games. They want to see intense rivals battling back and forth for a championship with the decision in doubt until the end, often including a come-from-behind win.

These 12 fights represent the best of MMA. They're the ones that fans remember, the ones that got them to their feet to shower fighters with standing ovations.

ROYCE GRACIE VS. KIMO (1994)

Royce Gracie dominated the first two UFC tournaments. He needed less than five minutes combined to win three fights at UFC 1. He then took less than nine minutes at UFC 2. He was the favorite again at UFC 3. His opening-round opponent was the inexperienced Hawaiian brawler Kimo. Gracie attacked but was unable to take down Kimo. When Gracie tried a judo takedown from against the cage, Kimo used his 50-pound (23 kg) weight advantage to come out on top. But Kimo could do little to submit or hurt the skilled Brazilian.

Royce Gracie is hoisted into the air after his victory match at UFC 1 in 1993.

Gracie reserved position, but only for a moment. Kimo regained control. Then Gracie grabbed Kimo's hair and threw short punches that bloodied Kimo's face. The fighters returned to their feet. Kimo again took down the smaller fighter, but this time, Gracie got the position he wanted. He locked Kimo's arm between his legs and submitted Kimo at the 4:40 mark. As the crowd roared, Kimo lay on his back unable to move. Meanwhile, Gracie needed to be helped to his feet as the event's announcers declared it the greatest fight in UFC history.

MARK COLEMAN VS. MAURICE SMITH (1997)

Wrestler Mark Coleman was the innovator of the ground-and-pound style, in which a fighter brings an opponent to the ground and dishes out punishment from above. At UFC 14, Coleman faced kickboxer Maurice Smith, who had no grappling experience and a losing MMA record. It seemed as though it was the perfect way to prove that wrestling expertise was critical to the success of future fighters.

Maurice Smith after winning a fight in 2007

Coleman dominated early. He easily took down Smith and pounded him with fists and head butts (which were legal at the time). Smith assumed a defensive position on his back, known as pulling guard. He locked up Coleman's body movement with his legs and diminished Coleman's power. By the nine-minute mark, Coleman was exhausted. He stood with his hands down and feet still, while Smith bounced as he threw strikes. Just before the end of regulation time (15 minutes), Smith threw a series of kicks to Coleman's legs that rocked the weary wrestler.

At the time, UFC rules called for overtime. So the fight continued. Coleman could barely defend himself and offered few attacks. Smith was also tired and couldn't knock out Coleman, but he continued to score with strikes. A second overtime saw more of the same, including a powerful head kick that staggered Coleman. In a huge upset, the judges declared Smith the new champion.

FRANK SHAMROCK VS. TITO ORTIZ (1999)

The UFC 22 battle between Tito Ortiz and Frank Shamrock was a classic. Ortiz, who bulked up between the weigh-in and the fight, used his weight advantage to ground and pound Shamrock. But Shamrock stayed busy on the bottom, blocking blows, pulling guards, and firing back with shots of his own. In the third round, Shamrock rocked Ortiz with leg kicks but was again taken down. This time, Ortiz landed a heavy knee while Shamrock was down (then legal). The knee cut Shamrock above the

eye. Ortiz used his fingers to rip at the cut!

Shamrock battled back early in the fourth round. He nailed the tired Ortiz with kick after kick until Ortiz's legs were a mass of welts. Ortiz pushed through the pain and fatigue to take Shamrock down, but on the ground, Shamrock punished Ortiz. Ortiz escaped but got locked in a guillotine choke. Shamrock delivered a barrage of elbows and punches that ended the fight at 4:45 of the fourth round. While Ortiz entered the UFC Hall of Fame, Shamrock retired as champion. Shamrock never again fought in the UFC, even though this 1999 classic was voted fight of the year.

RANDY COUTURE VS. PEDRO RIZZO (2001)

UFC 31 in 2001 was the first under new ownership with Dana White as president. Fans were looking for something big, and they got it in a 25-minute instant classic. Like many great MMA fights, it was a clash of styles. Couture, the reigning UFC heavyweight champ, had a background in wrestling and boxing. The Brazilian Pedro Rizzo was known for his BJJ and kickboxing skills.

Couture took control of the first round with a ground-and-pound approach. The second round was all Rizzo, who avoided another takedown and launched an assault of strikes. Couture scored an impressive takedown in the third round and kept up the pressure. While unable to finish Rizzo, Couture was in control all of round 4 and most of round 5. Near the end of the battle, as the fighters stood, a hard Rizzo kick knocked Couture down but not out. Despite the impressive finish, the judges declared Couture the winner. It was a unanimous, though controversial, decision.

MIRKO FILIPOVIC VS. ANTONIO RODRIGO NOGUEIRA (2003)

The main event at Pride Final Conflict 2003 was a classic case of the unstoppable force meeting the immovable object. Going into the fight, Croatian Mirko Filipovic was undefeated in Pride. He'd also won his last three fights in less than six minutes with devastating strikes. Meanwhile, Brazil's Antonio Rodrigo Nogueira had suffered just a single loss, to the legendary Fedor Emelianenko.

The two fought in front of 70,000 Japanese fans for the Pride heavyweight title. The big Croatian dominated the first 10-minute round. He pounded Nogueira with right jabs, left hooks, and vicious kicks. Just as the round was ending, Filipovic sent Nogueira to the mat with his most powerful kick yet. It seemed over for the Brazilian, but he was saved by the bell.

The second round started out much the same. Then Nogueira muscled Filipovic to the mat. Filipovic extended his left arm as he tried to push himself off the mat. In a flash, Nogueira snatched the arm, wrapped it between his legs, and pulled hard. Filipovic had no choice but to submit to the painful arm bar. After nearly 15 minutes spent on the defensive, Nogueira's toughness and heart earned him an upset victory.

FORREST GRIFFIN VS. STEPHAN BONNAR (2005)

Most great fights feature legendary fighters with lots of experience. But this fight saw two unknowns battling for a UFC contract as finalists on the first season of *The Ultimate Fighter*. Griffin and Bonnar left the crowd gasping for air with 15 minutes of bell-to-bell action that many consider to be one of the best fights in UFC history.

Griffin won the first round using leg kicks. Bonnar recovered in the second. A hard jab opened a cut on Griffin's nose, but the fight continued. Both fighters landed powerful combinations of strikes in the third round, but neither would go down. While Griffin won the fight by unanimous decision, the real winner was the UFC as fans tuned in to watch this epic battle. Dana White later called it the "most important fight in UFC history."

FEDOR EMELIANENKO VS. MIRKO FILIPOVIC (2005)

Pride's two best heavyweights battled it out in this classic bout. Russian sambo expert Fedor Emelianenko was Pride's undefeated heavyweight champion. Mirko Filipovic was dangerous because of his world-class kickboxing skills.

Fedor Emelianenko, 2010

Emelianenko was not intimidated. He took the action to Filipovic from the moment they entered the ring (Pride did not use a cage). He was dominating both on his feet and on the ground. But one Filipovic head kick sent the champ through the ropes, while a hard right staggered him.

Emelianenko controlled rounds 2 and 3 with solid strikes and takedowns, but he couldn't finish off Filipovic. The challenger fought back with hard kicks—any one of which could have ended the fight or even the champ's career. But none of the kicks landed squarely, and both fighters were still standing—bloody and exhausted—at the fight's end. The referee raised Emelianenko's hand in victory. *Sports Illustrated* later named their battle the fight of the decade.

GEORGES ST-PIERRE VS. B. J. PENN (2006)

UFC 58 marked former welterweight champion B. J. Penn's return to UFC. Penn was looking for a shot to reclaim that title. But there was a problem—a 170-pound (77 kg) problem named Georges St-Pierre—standing in his way. St-Pierre was an up-and-coming Canadian known for his aggressive style. UFC 58 pitted the two challengers up against each other for the right to a title shot.

Penn appeared as strong as ever at the start of the three-round fight. He landed several vicious strikes in the first minute. While St-Pierre survived the round, his face looked more like he'd survived a car crash! When Penn tried to press the action at the start of the second round, St-Pierre held him off with leg kicks until the Canadian finally scored a takedown. The two BJJ experts battled on the ground with Penn unable to reverse or sweep. Penn managed to get back to his feet, but before he could land a strike to gain back control, St-Pierre scored a takedown just seconds before the end of the round.

By the third round, Penn showed signs of tiring. St-Pierre kept shooting takedowns and throwing hard kicks. A hard slam on a single-leg takedown knocked the wind—and maybe the fight—out of Penn. St-Pierre was declared the winner in a split decision that many in the audience jeered. For Penn, the fight marked the start of a decline, while St-Pierre won the championship in his next fight and went on to become one of the best of all time.

CHUCK LIDDELL VS. WANDERLEI SILVA (2007)

This was a dream match between two men who were the best light heavyweights in the world for most of their careers. Liddell dominated the UFC, while Silva tore up Pride. By 2007 neither held the championship. Both were past their peak, but fans were still eager to see the legends battle it out. The two fighters had aggressive, exciting styles and huge fan followings.

Thirty seconds into the fight, both fighters started throwing bombs. They weren't simple punches or strikes but knockout-power rights and lefts with the occasional kick. Liddell won the round, but Silva won the crowd with his courage and toughness in taking Liddell's best shots and staying on his feet. The second round was a back-and-forth brawl that left the fighters and the audience spent.

The final round proved just as epic until Liddell tagged Silva with a surprising spinning back fist, which led to a hard takedown. Liddell won the fight by unanimous decision while many MMA publications named the clash 2007's Fight of the Year.

BROCK LESNAR VS. FRANK MIR (2009)

One of the advantages in professional wrestling is that promoters can arrange events to set up feuds and pick the most profitable time for a championship fight. UFC promoters don't often get that chance. But the timing was perfect for one of the biggest MMA events in history—UFC 100. There, former wrestling champ Brock Lesnar faced off against Frank Mir, the man who had defeated him in his UFC debut.

Lesnar and Mir's heavyweight title fight was the biggest story of UFC 100. Both men claimed the title, and the fight would finally settle it. Mir launched plenty of trash talk at Lesnar in the days leading up to the fight. Once the bell rang, however, Lesnar dominated. He scored one hard takedown after another and then pounded Mir on the ground. At one point, Lesnar locked Mir in something similar to a pro wrestling side headlock and landed punch after punch.

It was more of the same in the second round. At the 1:38 mark, referee Herb Dean had seen enough and called the fight with Lesnar as the winner. While it was not the most competitive MMA fight ever, the Lesnar vs. Mir rematch was the most profitable ever. It drew a sellout crowd of 10,871, earned $5 million, and attracted a then-record PPV audience of 1.6 million.

DAN HENDERSON VS. MAURÍCIO RUA (2011)

By the time light heavyweights Dan Henderson and Maurício Rua first fought in 2011, both were legends in the sport. They'd each held MMA championships in all three major organizations (UFC, Pride, and Strikeforce). At the time of the fight, Henderson was 40 years old and on his third return to the UFC. Rua was 10 years younger.

The battle between legends more than lived up to its billing. It wasn't merely a great fight. Dana White called it one of the greatest MMA fights of all time.

In the first round, Henderson gained control using hard strikes that dazed Rua and allowed Henderson to take him down. Henderson continued to inflict damage in the second round. Rua was a bloody mess, but Henderson couldn't put him away.

Fans watched in awe as the two men fought into the late rounds. This was no street fight. It was more like two athlete-artists painting a masterpiece.

Rua tried to end the fight early in round 5. He brought Henderson to the mat and pummeled him with punches and elbows. But before Rua could finish Henderson, the bell rang. Both fighters were so tired that they could barely stand for the decision—a victory for Henderson.

ANDERSON SILVA VS. CHAEL SONNEN (2011)

Chael Sonnen's interviews leading up to his challenge to Silva's light heavyweight championship were trash talk at its best (or worst). Going into the fight, all the advantages seemed to be for unbeaten Silva. Sonnen's only hope seemed to be his wrestling skills.

Yet it was strikes, not grappling, that dominated most of the fight. Sonnen struck Silva's body and face nearly 300 times. It was estimated to be the most ever in a UFC fight and perhaps as many as Silva had absorbed in his entire MMA career!

Sonnen won the battle on his feet. Once on the ground, he pounded away. Silva attempted submissions from guard, but Sonnen fought them off. Although Silva landed some hard elbows and opened a cut on Sonnen's forehead, Sonnen controlled the first four rounds.

By the fifth and final round, the crowd, which had jeered the trash-talking Sonnen during the introductions, was behind him. Sonnen gained another takedown. But with lightning quickness, Silva wrapped Sonnen's arm and neck in between his own legs. Sonnen tried to fight but could not escape this triangle choke hold. Halfway through the round, he was forced to tap out. Their 2012 rematch proved to be a huge moneymaker with the same result, this time in the second round.

SANTOS VS. CARANO

In Strikeforce, men weren't the only stars. Women also battled it out in the ring. Two women stood out among all others: Gina Carano and Cris Santos. Santos made a name for herself with her charisma, while Carano's fitness model appeal gained the attention of many male fans. Yet they were more than show, they were also skilled. Both were undefeated in their professional careers.

Their August 15, 2009, fight was historic on several levels. It was the first main event on a major MMA show to feature women. It was also the fight that would crown the first female champion. The response was just as historic: a sellout crowd of almost 14,000 and the highest ratings for an MMA event on Showtime. MMA fans on the Internet buzzed over the match. For a time, Carano and Santos were the most searched subjects on Yahoo and the most discussed topic on Twitter.

But the fight itself didn't live up to expectations. The Brazilian Santos overwhelmed American Carano. With one minute left in the first round, Santos grounded Carano and began pounding. Carano tried to defend, but Santos's strikes came fast and furious. The ref called the fight with one second left! Santos gained the victory, and women's MMA won as the two proved that women could draw an audience as well as men could.

Gina Carano (left) and Cris Santos (right) trade punches in a Strikeforce championship match in 2009.

4 KINGS OF THE CAGE:
GREATS OF MMA

Thousands of men and women have participated in MMA at the amateur or professional levels. Some fight only a few times. Others make it a career. A select few become legends. These 17 fighters represent the best of the best. Many are in the UFC Hall of Fame, while the others are bound for that honor. They've combined brain and brawn to become true kings of the cage!

MARK "THE HAMMER" COLEMAN (1964–)

Like Dan Severn, Coleman brought outstanding amateur wrestling credentials to MMA. Among them was a seventh-place finish in freestyle at the 100 kg (220-pound) weight class at the 1992 Summer Olympics. Coleman entered the UFC in 1996 with a bang, winning tournaments at both UFC 10 and 11 and then submitting Dan Severn at UFC 12 to become the first UFC heavyweight champion. Coleman is known as the Godfather of Ground and Pound because of his success pioneering that style.

Mark Coleman *(left)* takes a hit from Maurício Rua in a 2009 fight in Ireland.

Coleman peaked early. After UFC 12, he lost his title in his next fight, lost two more fights, and then left the UFC. He went to Pride, and while he lost his debut, he came back to win his next six fights. In 2008 Coleman was inducted into the UFC Hall of Fame. The next year, the Hammer was back in the UFC ring for the first time in a decade. In 2010 he defeated fellow Hall of Famer Randy Couture, grounding and pounding his way to another victory.

RANDY "THE NATURAL" COUTURE (1963–)

Randy Couture is a walking MMA record book. A few of his honors include most championship reigns, most championship fights, and the first fighter to hold championships in two weight classes.

A world-class amateur wrestler, the Natural was a three-time NCAA All-American and a three-time Olympic alternate. He also boxed and wrestled while serving in the U.S. Army. He debuted at UFC 13 in 1997 and retired after UFC 129 in 2011. In between, he headlined more UFC fights than anyone. He won his last title at the age of 43! His UFC 91 main event against Brock Lesnar was the first UFC PPV to draw more than 1 million viewers.

Couture innovated the style called dirty boxing, in which he would clinch onto his opponent and hammer him with strikes. He was named to the UFC Hall of Fame in 2006.

FEDOR "THE LAST EMPEROR" EMELIANENKO (1976–)

Many experts list Fedor Emelianenko as the greatest fighter in MMA history. The Russian won international sambo and judo tournaments before turning to MMA. In 2000 he lost his fifth professional fight in a controversial decision. He didn't lose another for 10 years. During that decade of dominance, the tough Russian defeated many other MMA legends. In 2003 he beat Antonio Rodrigo Nogueira to win the Pride Heavyweight Championship, a title he never lost. *Sports Illustrated* named him the fighter of the decade. His 2005 victory over Mirko Filipovic was the fight of the decade. And his 2009 KO of former UFC heavyweight champion Andrei Arlovski was the knockout of the decade.

The fighter called the Last Emperor defeated many UFC fighters. But he never actually competed in the UFC. A hero to Russian fans, Emelianenko served as one of his nation's torchbearers at the 2008 Summer Olympics, the only MMA fighter ever to be so honored.

RASHAD "SUGA" EVANS (1979–)

Trained by MMA legend Dan Severn, Evans won the second season of *The Ultimate Fighter*. He continued his winning ways with 10 straight victories until he fought to a draw against Tito Ortiz at UFC 73 in 2007. In 2008 Evans won the knockout of the year honor for his KO of Chuck Liddell. He then won the light heavyweight title from Forrest Griffin—a dream match that featured the winners of the first two seasons of *The Ultimate Fighter*.

Rashad Evans *(left, in blue)* jabs at Rogerio Nogueira in a fight in 2013.

Evans lost the title a year later at the main event of UFC 98. It was the first of many main events for Evans. He bounced back from the loss with four straight wins until bowing to MMA phenom Jon "Bones" Jones in 2012. Though trained as a wrestler, Evans's striking ability is well known, and his fists are anything but sweet as "suga" for his foes.

MIRKO "CRO COP" FILIPOVIC (1974–)

Any MMA highlight reel is bound to feature Filipovic's devastating head kick knockouts. A member of an elite Croatian special forces team, Filipovic was dubbed Cro Cop. After enjoying great success in kickboxing, Filipovic struggled at first in MMA. But his win over MMA legend Kazushi Sakuraba in 2002 marked the beginning of Filipovic's domination of the Pride heavyweight division. He became known for quick knockout victories, often from head kicks. Even his losses were impressive. Antonio Rodrigo Nogueira and Fedor Emelianenko each beat Filipovic in bouts later named fight of the year.

Mirko Filipovic punches his opponent, Eddie Sanchez, in the face in 2007.

Filipovic made his UFC debut at UFC 67. While he failed to achieve the same success in UFC, his striking ability still made him dangerous. In an interview, Cro Cop described his fighting philosophy: "Right leg, hospital; left leg, cemetery."

WEIGHING IN

The Unified Rules of Mixed Martial Arts designate limits for nine different weight classes. Fighters tyically fight in the lightest weight class for which they qualify.

Flyweight: up to 125 pounds (57 kg)
Bantamweight: up to 135 pounds (61 kg)
Featherweight: up to 145 pounds (66 kg)
Lightweight: up to 155 pounds (70 kg)
Welterweight: up to 170 pounds (77 kg)
Middleweight: up to 185 pounds (84 kg)
Light Heavyweight: up to 205 pounds
   (93 kg)
Heavyweight: up to 265 pounds (120 kg)
Super Heavyweight: more than 265
   pounds (120 kg)

The UFC crowns champions in all but the super heavyweight division.

RICH "ACE" FRANKLIN (1974–)

Franklin came to MMA later in life, after working as a high school teacher—where, presumably, no students ever challenged him! Franklin made his MMA debut in 1999 and UFC debut in 2001, but it wasn't until 2005 that he really made his name with a first-round knockout of UFC legend Ken Shamrock. In his next fight, he captured the UFC middleweight title for the first time.

Nicknamed Ace for his resemblance to actor Jim Carey (star of the 1994 movie *Ace Ventura: Pet Detective),* Franklin has fought his share of ace fighters, including 10 battles against current or former UFC and Pride champions. The former teacher served as coach for seasons 2 and 11 of *The Ultimate Fighter.* He also shared his knowledge in the book *The Complete Idiot's Guide to Ultimate Fighting.*

ROYCE GRACIE (1966–)

Dana White described Royce Gracie as "the Godfather . . . we all bow down and kiss the ring of Royce." The son of MMA pioneer and BJJ inventor Helio Gracie, Royce competed in his first jiu-jitsu tournament at the age of eight. He compiled an amateur record of 51–3.

Gracie dominated the early UFC, winning three matches in one night to win tournaments at UFC 1, 2, and 4. He won each of these fights in less than five minutes.

Gracie left the UFC in 1995, citing disagreements with rule changes. He did not fight again until 2000, when he lost an epic 90-minute battle with Kazushi Sakuraba. Gracie was inducted into the UFC Hall of Fame in 2005. He returned to the cage a year later and suffered his first UFC loss. Even into his mid-40s, Gracie has hinted at a future comeback.

DANGEROUS DAN HENDERSON (1970–)

With handfuls of gold medals in international amateur wrestling, Henderson was a lock for MMA success. He debuted at UFC 17 in 1998 and won the middleweight title. In 2011 Henderson's unanimous decision over Maurício Rua at UFC 139 was named 2011 fight of the year.

In between, Henderson beat some of the best in UFC and other promotions while fighting at three different weight classes. Although Dangerous Dan came from a wrestling background, his right hand is called the H-Bomb because of its power. Henderson can take a punch as well. In his 15-year career, he has never lost a fight by knockout or technical knockout.

Dan Henderson celebrates a win over Fedor Emelianenko in 2011.

MATT HUGHES (1973–)

Matt Hughes was a two-time NCAA All-American in wrestling before he turned to MMA. He quickly became a force in the Octagon. From 1998 to 2000, he won 16 straight fights. He captured the welterweight title in 2001 as part of a streak of 13 straight wins. One in that streak was a victory over Carlos Newton at UFC 34 in their famous double knockout.

After losing the welterweight title in 2004, he quickly regained it by defeating Georges St-Pierre in the first round at UFC 50. He ran off another six-fight win streak until St-Pierre regained the title at UFC 65 in 2006. When Hughes entered the UFC Hall of Fame in 2010, he ranked number 1 all time in UFC wins and fights finished, and ranked number 2 in most fights.

CHUCK "THE ICEMAN" LIDDELL (1969–)

No fighter in UFC has more knockouts than Chuck Liddell (23)—and many of those came against fellow UFC legends. In his series of fights with Tito Ortiz and Randy Couture, Liddell lost the first fight but came back to win the rematch against each fighter. During his prime, Liddell was the most dominant UFC fighter in history and probably the most famous. He starred in the first season of *The Ultimate Fighter* in 2005. He was also the first UFC fighter featured on the cover of a national sports magazine (*ESPN the Magazine* in 2007).

Chuck Liddell *(left)* fights Rashad "Suga" Evans at UFC 88 in 2008.

At the height of his fame, Liddell lost his title at UFC 71 to Rampage Jackson. Liddell went on to lose, by knockout, four of his final five matches. As much as for his fights, Liddell will be remembered for his frantic post-match celebrations that remain a staple of UFC highlight reels.

ANTONIO "BIG NOG" RODRIGO NOGUEIRA (1976–)

Antonio Nogueira *(right)* is one of only three men to have held titles in both Pride and UFC. The Brazilian-born jiu-jitsu specialist started his career in Japan with the Rings promotion. He later moved to Pride and in 2001 became the promotion's first heavyweight champion. He held the title until 2004, when he lost to Fedor Emelianenko. That loss remained his only defeat in Pride until 2006.

Big Nog brought his toughness and skill to UFC in 2007. In just his second fight, he won the interim (temporary) UFC heavyweight championship. (This title was created as a placeholder until Randy Couture, who had recently left UFC, decided to return.) His 2009 unanimous-decision victory at UFC 102 over Couture was named Fight of the Year.

TITO "THE HUNTINGTON BEACH BAY BOY" ORTIZ (1975–)

When Ortiz retired after UFC 148 in 2012, he left behind a legacy that few can match, combining tremendous success in the Octagon and an outrageous personality. His UFC records include most UFC fights, most light heavyweight championship fights, and most fights won.

The Californian started off as a sparring partner for early UFC tough-guy Tank Abbott. From Abbott, he learned the art of being colorful. This helped make him one of the breakout stars of the early UFC.

Ortiz earned his nickname with feuds against fellow MMA legends Chuck Liddell and Ken Shamrock, as well as his ability to stir up controversy. His 2002 fight against Shamrock at UFC 40 helped to save the promotion, and their high-profile rematches in 2006 pushed UFC into the limelight. But 2006 ended on a down note as Ortiz lost to Chuck Liddell for the second time and soon after left UFC. Ortiz struggled upon his return in 2007, but he still remained one of the best-known fighters in the UFC.

Above: Tito Ortiz lands a head kick on Forrest Griffin in a bout in 2009. *Below:* Kazushi Sakuraba attempts to put MMA great Royce Gracie into a submission hold in 2007.

KAZUSHI "THE GRACIE HUNTER" SAKURABA (1969–)

After successful high school and college wrestling careers, Sakuraba joined the pro game. While trained to work an entertaining match, Sakuraba also learned catch-wrestling techniques. He showed he was the real deal when he joined Pride and won the Ultimate Japan tournament in 1997.

His biggest victory came two years later over the previously undefeated Royler Gracie at Pride 8. Royler's

brother Royce sought revenge at Pride Grand Prix 2000. Under a special set of rules that included no time limit, the two battled for an epic 90 minutes until the Gracie family threw in the towel (conceded defeat). Sakuraba also defeated Renzo and Ryan Gracie. He would meet his match, not with a Gracie family member but with another BJJ black belt, Wanderlei Silva, in 2001. Sakuraba also lost two rematches to Silva as years of punishment took their toll. While never the best in the world, he drew some of the largest crowds in MMA history as the Gracie Hunter and became a hero in Japan.

KEN "THE WORLD'S MOST DANGEROUS MAN" SHAMROCK (1964–)

Shamrock was one of three pro wrestlers to form Pancrase in Japan in 1993. While the events were promoted like pro wrestling, most of the fights were real. Shamrock dominated, winning the King of Pancrase title. With his charisma and muscled physique, he became an early icon of MMA. He fought at UFC 1 but lost to Royce Gracie. A 1995 rematch to determine the first UFC championship ended in a draw (at that time, there were no judges). At UFC 6, Shamrock became champion by defeating Dan Severn, only to lose the title to Severn at UFC 9 in 1996.

After UFC 9, Shamrock left for WWE but continued to train fighters. After one of his fighters lost

Ken Shamrock *(left)* heads into the ring for a fight in 2006.

to Tito Ortiz at UFC 19, Shamrock was enraged by Ortiz's disrespectful actions. Their hugely successful fight at UFC 40 in 2002 played a big part in saving the UFC. The two acted as opposing coaches for the third season of *The Ultimate Fighter*. They then took their feud into the cage at UFC 61 in 2006, which set new PPV records. Their third fight, a few months later, drew record TV ratings for MMA. Shamrock was one of the first two members of the UFC Hall of Fame.

ANDERSON "THE SPIDER" SILVA (1975–)

UFC president Dana White once called Silva *(left)* the best pound-for-pound fighter in the world. As of 2012, Silva held a number of UFC records. They include the longest UFC win streak (15 matches), best all-time UFC win percentage (90 percent), most title fight victories (10), and the longest title reign (more than 2,100 days).

Silva began his career in his native Brazil but won his first championship in Japan's Shooto promotion in 2001. He won his UFC debut in 2006 in just 49 seconds! At UFC 64, he captured the UFC middleweight championship. Silva's long limbs and small torso have earned him the nickname the Spider. He is a precision striker with a strong chin— meaning he can take a punch as well as he can deliver one.

WANDERLEI "THE AXE MURDERER" SILVA (1976–)

After losing two of his first three UFC fights, Silva moved to Pride. There he dominated the middleweight division for four years. He was unbeaten in 18 fights from 2000 to 2004. His only draw during that span came against heavyweight Mirko Filipovic. Three of Silva's wins came over Kazushi Sakuraba, and two KO wins were over Rampage Jackson. Silva holds numerous Pride records including most wins and knockouts, longest win streak, and most title defenses.

Silva trained with fellow BJJ great Anderson Silva (no relation) and Maurício Rua, and coached *The Ultimate Fighter: Brazil* show in 2012. Even though the Axe Murderer holds a black belt in BJJ, it is his strikes and intensity that make him a surefire Hall of Famer.

Wanderlei Silva in May 2008

GEORGES "GSP" ST-PIERRE (1981–)

As a boy in Quebec, Canada, St-Pierre studied karate to defend himself from a school bully. His interest soon spread to BJJ, wrestling, and boxing. The skills he learned from these sports form the backbone of GSP's style.

After a series of wins at the start of his UFC career, St-Pierre lost to Matt Hughes in his first attempt to capture the welterweight

Georges St-Pierre throws a fierce punch at Jake Shields in UFC 129 (2011).

title. He defeated Hughes in a 2006 rematch to win the title. He then lost a stunning upset to Matt Serra a year later. It was his last defeat. GSP regained the title and ran off a series of victories, most by unanimous decision. Hailed as the greatest Canadian MMA fighter of all time, GSP headlined UFC 129 in Toronto in 2011. More than 50,000 fans packed the Rogers Centre to watch him successfully defend his welterweight title.

RISING STARS

With *The Ultimate Fighter* TV show as a training ground, as well as small MMA promotions around the world, new MMA stars are always rising. Two of the brightest were born just a few years before UFC 1 in 1993.

Jon Jones *(above)* and Junior Dos Santos *(facing)* are two of MMA's up-and-coming stars.

JON "BONES" JONES (1987–)

With only four months of professional experience, Jones debuted in the UFC at the age of 20. He won the light heavyweight title at the age of 23. Although his background is in wrestling, Jones is best known for his striking ability and his skill at knocking out opponents. Jones strikes not only with power and precision but with creativity, using uncommon moves such as spinning back fists.

Jones suffered his only MMA defeat in 2009, when he was disqualified for using illegal elbow strikes. He bounced back to dominate the UFC light heavyweight division. He handed Rampage Jackson his first loss by submission at UFC 135 in 2011.

Jones then won a unanimous decision over his friend and former training partner Rashad Evans at UFC 145 in 2012. With his skill and youth, many experts believe Bones Jones is on the road to MMA greatness.

JUNIOR "JDS" DOS SANTOS (1984–)

Junior Dos Santos represents the next generation of MMA fighters. Unlike earlier fighters, most of whom trained in one style and then cross-trained in others, Dos Santos trained for MMA at an early age. He said he had dreamed of fighting in the UFC since he was a child.

Dos Santos burst onto the scene with power, winning his first five pro fights. After a loss, he reeled off 10 more victories, eight of them by KO or TKO. He captured the UFC heavyweight title in 2011 with a first-round knockout of Cain Velasquez at *UFC on Fox 1*. Dos Santos's combination of power and skill has earned him praise from MMA experts, many of whom believe he is the future of MMA.

Junior Dos Santos poses during his weigh-in for a fight in 2011.

5 *EXCITEMENT UNCAGED:*
EIGHT MEMORABLE MOMENTS IN MMA HISTORY

Like any sport, MMA has a rich history filled with skilled athletes engaging in dramatic competition. Similar to those other sports, it is not always the entire game or bout that fans remember but instead one special moment. Below are eight for the MMA highlight reel of jaw-dropping action.

DOUBLE KO: MATT HUGHES VS. CARLOS NEWTON (2001)

What if two fighters simultaneously knocked each other out? It happened at UFC 34, where a match of power vs. skill brought on an unforgettable UFC first.

Carlos Newton was defending his welterweight title against Matt Hughes. Hughes was known for his hard takedowns, while Newton was a submission expert. Early in the second round, Hughes slammed Newton hard to the mat. But he exposed his neck as he leaned over the champ. Newton quickly raised his legs and wrapped them tightly around Hughes's neck in a triangle choke. Hughes picked up Newton from the mat so that Newton was almost sitting on Hughes's shoulders. He then rammed Newton's back into the cage. But the champ wouldn't let go. With one last

Matt Hughes *(right)* and Carlos Newton *(left)* met again in 2002 in London. Known as the "Brawl in the Royal Albert Hall," it was the first UFC event to be held outside of the United States. Hughes won the fight against Newton for a second time.

gasp, Hughes slammed Newton to the mat. The force of the blow knocked out Newton, causing referee Big John McCarthy to stop the fight. What McCarthy didn't see was that Hughes had been choked unconscious. It was a pretty good slam from Hughes, considering he was asleep!

THE SAITAMA SLUGFEST: DON FRYE VS. YOSHIHIRO TAKAYAMA (2002)

When MMA began, critics compared it to hockey brawls where two unskilled fighters swung away. A 2002 Pride fight at the Saitama Super Arena in Japan between Don "the Predator" Frye and Japanese pro wrestler Yoshihiro Takayama brought that very image to life. Throughout the fight, each fighter clung to the back of the other's neck, trading rapid-fire punches. The crowd was frenzied. So was announcer Bas Rutten, who declared that he'd never seen anything like it.

While Takayama mixed in body shots, the Predator was head-hunting. Three times during the fight, the two stood toe-to-toe throwing bombs, neither bothering to defend. After a takedown, Frye pounded Takayama with shot after shot until the referee ended the fight after just over 6:00 minutes in round 1. (Pride had 10-minute rounds.) Takayama could barely stand, and both of his eyes were swollen shut. The Saitama slugfest remains one of the most watched MMA fights on YouTube.

MMA POWER BOMB:
BOB SAPP VS. ANTONIO RODRIGO NOGUEIRA (2002)

Antonio Nogueira's nickname, Big Nog, comes not just from his huge size but to distinguish him from his light heavyweight twin brother of the same name. But Nog, at 6 feet 3 inches (1.9 meters), 240 pounds (109 kg), didn't look so big against 6-foot-5-inch (2 m), 325-pound (147 kg) Bob "the Beast" Sapp. Sapp's first two fights had been quick knockout wins. His style was to rush his opponents and throw hard punches. Nogueira had battled and beaten many skilled fighters. But he'd never challenged anyone who towered over him and outweighed him by nearly 100 pounds (45 kg).

When Big Nog tried a takedown, Sapp stuffed it. Where most fighters would have smothered Nogueira, Sapp instead picked him up, holding Nogueira upside down with his feet above Sapp's head! In a move that reminded many of the pro wrestling move called a power bomb, Sapp slammed Big Nog's noggin hard onto the mat. Although Sapp tried to finish the BJJ expert with hard punches, Nogueira fought his way free. By the end of the first 10-minute round, Sapp appeared exhausted. Early in the second, Big Nog snatched Sapp's arm in a submission hold, and the Beast was slain, despite having delivered one beautiful bomb.

THE RANDLEPLEX:
KEVIN RANDLEMAN VS. FEDOR EMELIANENKO (2004)

Few have entered MMA with a better wrestling background than Kevin Randleman. He'd been one of the nation's top wrestlers at Ohio State University. In 2004 he entered the Pride heavyweight tournament. As one of the only experienced wrestlers competing, Randleman's chances looked bright until he ran into Fedor Emelianenko. Emelianenko wasn't just the Pride heavyweight champion, he was an MMA demolition machine.

Within the first minute of the fight, Randleman almost broke the machine in half. Randleman controlled on the ground, and as Emelianenko escaped and started to stand, the American wrapped his hands around the Russian's waist. With a mighty heave, Randleman lifted Emelianenko high in the air, almost over his head, and slammed the champ neck first onto the mat! The Russian's neck hit the mat at a terrible angle, and many watching thought that it must be broken. But Emelianenko was fine. His neck—and his spirit—remained strong. Just seconds later, the champ was back in control, forcing a submission from Randleman.

DOWN AND OUT: WANDERLEI SILVA VS. RAMPAGE JACKSON (2004)

Silva had defeated Jackson by TKO in November 2003 in a controversial first encounter. Jackson, unhappy with the officiating during that fight, demanded a rematch. Perhaps he should have been careful what he wished for!

Their bout at Pride 28 saw an evenly matched first round, until Silva connected with a powerful right jab that sent Jackson toward the ropes. (Pride used boxing ropes, not a cage.) Before Rampage could recover, Silva grabbed Jackson in a clinch and rammed four knee strikes into his face. The last strike knocked Jackson through the ring ropes, unconscious and with blood pouring from his face. He was the victim of one of the most graphic knockout moments in MMA history.

TKO OF GSP: MATT SERRA VS. GEORGES ST-PIERRE (2007)

Canadian welterweight Georges St-Pierre had just avenged his only MMA loss by defeating Matt Hughes to capture the welterweight title at UFC 65. He faced Matt Serra in his first title defense. Most experts favored GSP to win the match. Even as the fighters were entering the cage for the main event, the TV announcers were wondering who would next challenge GSP for his title.

Those who expected a quick fight were correct. But they were wrong about the victor. The shorter Serra came out aggressively, and GSP couldn't hit the smaller target. As GSP moved in, Serra hit him with a hard right hook. Serra swarmed St-Pierre with strike after strike until referee John McCarthy had seen enough and waved his hands. It was over. A

TKO of GSP! In some ways, no result could've been better for the UFC. The rematch at UFC 83—the promotion's debut in Canada—set the record for fastest sellout and largest attendance. St-Pierre won the rematch, but UFC was the real winner.

KICKER GETS KICKED: MIRKO FILIPOVIC VS. GABRIEL GONZAGA (2007)

Any MMA highlight reel features Cro Cop's roundhouse KO kicks in the middle of a Pride ring. Of all the Pride fighters, Filipovic was perhaps the one that UFC fans most wanted to see in action. In his debut at UFC in February 2007, he had not disappointed with a quick TKO victory. His next UFC foe, BJJ expert Gabriel Gonzaga, was a heavy underdog. Experts felt his best chance was to get the big Croatian to the ground and submit him. But Gonzaga announced before the fight that he intended to stand toe-to-toe with the former kickboxing champ! Cro Cop replied that everyone has a plan until they get hit.

Early on, Filipovic tried to land his signature kicks, but Gonzaga defended with a takedown. On the ground, the BJJ black belt nailed Cro Cop repeatedly with elbows. Somewhat dazed, the former Pride champ returned to his feet, but before he could land his famous KO kick, Gonzaga unleashed one of his own. Cro Cop's knees buckled, and he hit the mat. It proved to be one of the great MMA upsets and knockouts of all time when the great kicker got kicked!

SNAP!: FRANK MIR VS. ANTONIO RODRIGO NOGUEIRA (2011)

Big Nog was no longer a dominant force when he squared off in a rematch against former UFC champion Frank Mir at UFC 140. The determined Brazilian showed no fear, trading strikes with Mir, almost daring Mir to try to knock him out. It would have been better for Big Nog if he'd taken one on the chin.

After Nogueira dropped Mir with two hard rights, the fight went to the mat. Rather than using his BJJ skills to submit Mir, Big Nog threw punches. Mir caught

Frank Mir *(top)* uses an arm bar to defeat Antonio Rodrigo Nogueira in their 2011 bout.

Nogueira's arm and locked on an arm bar. Desperate to escape, Nogueira tried rolling free, but Mir held tight. As they rolled on the mat, Mir got better position and applied a Kimura. Just as Maeda did 50 years earlier in his fight with Helio Gracie, the underdog Brazilian fought until he could take no more. It's unclear which sound fans heard first: the bell ringing or the snapping of Big Nog's arm breaking.

THE DANCE IN DETROIT

If these are some of the most memorable moments in MMA history, there are just as many to fill a list of worst moments in UFC history, including cheap shots, brawls after the fight, and crazy stunts. Perhaps the worst moment came early just as UFC was poised for a breakout and instead got a knockout that put fans to sleep. National reporters were on hand for UFC 9, a rematch between Dan Severn and UFC champion Ken Shamrock in Detroit in May 1996.

To put on the event, the UFC agreed to several rule changes, most important the outlawing of closed-fist strikes. Shamrock, already injured before the match, had his best weapon taken away against the grappler Severn. Severn had shown in his previous fights that while he might be nicknamed the Beast, his style was more careful. He was patient and waited for the right time to strike. But on that long night, nobody struck as the two fighters circled each other with little contact. The fans jeered in disappointment. While Severn and Shamrock didn't hurt each other during the Dance in Detroit, they did damage the image of the sport, not by making it seem too violent but by making it seem too boring.

6 EVOLUTION:
THE FUTURE OF MMA

The UFC has overcome the reputation for brutality that it once faced. But that doesn't mean it's accepted worldwide. The sport's violent nature still leads to many critics, and some states—including New York—still won't allow professional MMA fights.

The arguments against MMA have changed little in the past 20 years. Yet there have been no deaths or serious injuries to fighters in a major MMA promotion. Sadly, there have been tragedies in smaller promotions. MMA, however, keeps updating its rules to protect the fighters, while allowing them to use their full set of skills and entertain the audience.

Like all pro sports, MMA is competition, but it is also entertainment. One of the biggest knocks against Anderson Silva, perhaps the greatest MMA fighter ever, is that his fights are boring. The UFC does copy many of the tricks of the WWE, including theme music, interviews filled with trash talking, and endless merchandising. But any attempt to work fights to increase the entertainment factor would be the end of UFC and maybe MMA.

The UFC is positioned to continue to grow. It appears on a wide range of television channels, from broadcast networks to cable stations. But the results have been mixed. While some broadcast programs struggle to find viewership, top-level PPV events continue to be among the best selling in UFC history. Some experts believe the popularity of MMA has peaked and that overexposure on TV has burned out fans. Others believe that UFC's dominance of the sport is bad and that the lack of competition results in a bland product.

There are other possible strikes against MMA, in particular the UFC. Since UFC 3, when both Ken Shamrock and Royce Gracie had to pull out of matches because of injuries, the UFC has dealt with injuries to major fighters just as they were preparing for big fights. A related issue coming into focus concerns the long-term health effects of MMA. With football players suing the National Football League because of brain injuries, the UFC might face a similar suit. It is well known that many boxers have suffered long-term effects due to repeated punches to the head, but the sport of MMA is still too young to know what a career of taking strikes to the head will do. The very thing that makes the sport exciting might also lead to its downfall.

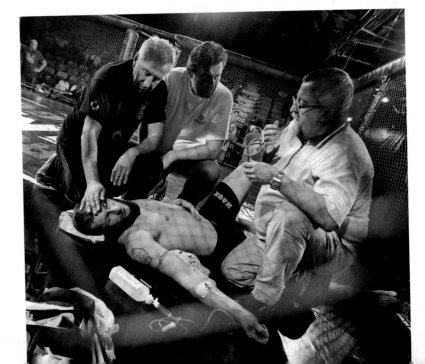

The safety of MMA fighters is a big concern. Karlo Trnar, pictured here, had to be rushed to the hospital after his 2012 bout with Mario Jagatic.

Vitor Belfort lands a kick on Michael Bisping during their 2013 bout.

Dana White's announced goal is to make the UFC the number one sport in the world. With its first event in China, the world's most populous country, in 2012, the UFC is on its way to becoming a true global brand. Past events held in Japan, Brazil, Germany, Ireland, and Great Britain have sold out within minutes. The growth of the UFC internationally has also led to copycat promotions. These promotions may not challenge the UFC for dominance but will instead serve as yet another training ground for UFC main event stars. Another major area of growth for UFC is its new women's division. In February

Ronda Rousey hurls a punch at Liz Carmouche in the woman's bantamweight championship in 2013. Rounsey won the bout in the first round.

2013, former Olympian Ronda Rousey won UFC's first women's title fight.

There are plenty of future mixed martial artists already as millions of kids in dojos are learning one martial art, then another and another, all with the goal of making it in the MMA. Those young people not only watch MMA but want to make it a career. Many young adults have turned their attention away from stars of other sports and view UFC stars as heroes. Twenty years ago, amateur wrestlers who wanted to make a living had no choice but to join the ranks of fake pro wrestling, while black belts in any martial art could only hope to find employment running a dojo. Now there is another option: the Octagon. With this global grassroots fan base, MMA will continue to flourish. MMA fighters may tap out, but the sport won't at any time in the near future.

DEALING WITH DRUGS

Like many pro sports, MMA faces a drug problem. Coming off his victory over Brock Lesnar, Alistair Overeem was set to fight Junior Dos Santos for the heavyweight title in May 2012. But then he tested positive for steroids. Hall of Famers like Ken Shamrock have failed drug tests, and even women's champion Cris Santos got caught using steroids. The UFC can suspend steroid users, but even the threat of suspension doesn't stop some fighters from abusing the drugs. Other fighters find their careers destroyed not by injuries in the ring but by addiction to painkillers. In such a physical and violent sport, drug abuse can be a big problem. Curbing drug use will be one of UFC's greatest challenges going forward.

GLOSSARY

brancaille: a combat sport based on wrestling but that allows strikes

Brazilian jiu-jitsu (BJJ): a martial art that focuses on grappling, in particular fighting on the ground. BJJ is also called Gracie jiu-jitsu.

catch wrestling: a wrestling style popular in the late 1800s that involved the use of any hold, including painful submission holds

choke: any hold used by a fighter around an opponent's throat with the goal of submission. A blood choke cuts off the supply of blood to the brain while an air choke restricts oxygen.

dojo: a martial arts school

gogoplata: a choke hold in which a fighter places his shin against a foe's throat

grappling: the act of using moves to control an opponent, either to get him to the mat or used once the opponent is on the mat. Wrestlers are often called grapplers.

ground and pound: a fighting style in which a fighter brings his opponent to the mat and then punishes him with strikes

guard: a defensive position used by a fighter on the mat. The grounded fighter uses his body to guard against blows and to control his opponent's body.

jeet kune do: a martial arts philosophy developed by martial arts expert Bruce Lee that combines techniques from a variety of martial arts

jiu-jitsu: a Japanese martial art that focuses on grappling rather than striking

joint hold: a submission hold, such as an arm bar, where pressure is applied to a joint in the human body, such as the knee or the shoulder

judo: a martial art that focuses on throws. Judo experts stress leverage and position over raw power.

karate: a martial art that features a wide range of strikes

kempo: a form of karate that features a series of quick movements in rapid succession

Kimura: a judo submission hold named after Japanese judo master Masahiko Kimura. The move is also known as ude-garami.

muay Thai: a combat sport from Thailand that features strikes and clinches. It is often referred as the Art of Eight Limbs for its use of knee, fist, elbow, and foot used both right- and left-handed.

Octagon: the eight-sided cage developed for the UFC

pankration: an early Olympic sport, in which combatants could both wrestle and box

sambo: a form of judo from Russia with an emphasis on grappling

shoot: in amateur wrestling, to attempt to take an opponent. In pro wrestling, shoot refers to anything that is real rather than predetermined.

sprawl and brawl: a strategy used to avoid takedown. A fighter sprawls his body away from an opponent who is attempting a takedown and also uses strikes to keep the fight from going to the mat.

strike: any blow, including punches, kicks, elbow strikes, and knee strikes

submission: a hold used for the purpose of making an opponent give up due to intense pain or fear of injury

tap out: to surrender, either by tapping the mat or one's opponent

technical knockout (TKO): a decision by a referee to end a fight because one fighter is no longer able to defend himself

vale tudo: an early "anything goes" combat sport from Brazil, popularized by the Gracie family

SOURCE NOTES

30 Dave Meltzer, "UFC's Greatest Hits: The Middle Years," Yahoo Sports, November 24, 2008, http://sports .yahoo.com/mma/news?slug=dm-ufcmiddle112408 (November 24, 2012).

39 Eric Kowal, "Mirko 'Cro Cop' Filipovic and the 5 Fights That Defined His Career," USCombatSports.com, October 31, 2011, http://uscombatsports.com/index.php?option=com_flexicontent&view=items&cid=228&id =9774&Itemid=56 (December 13, 2012).

40 Mixed Martial Arts, "UFC Announces Ultimate Royce Gracie," MixedMartialArts.com, n.d., http://www .mixedmartialarts.com/news/314349/UFC-announces-Ultimate-Royce-Gracie (December 1, 2012).

FURTHER READING

Books

Franklin, Rich. *The Complete Idiot's Guide to Ultimate Fighting.* New York: Alpha Books, 2007.

Gerbasi, Thomas. *UFC Encyclopedia: The Definitive Guide to the Ultimate Fighting Championship.* Indianapolis: BradyGames, 2011.

Hamilton, John. *Inside the Octagon.* Edina, MN: Abdo, 2011.

Jones, Patrick. *The Main Event: The Moves and Muscle of Pro Wrestling.* Minneapolis: Millbrook Press, 2013.

Savage, Jeff. *Brock Lesnar.* Greensboro, NC: Morgan Reynolds Pub., 2012.

Wells, Garrison. Martial Arts Sports Zone series. Minneapolis: Lerner Publications Company, 2012.

Wiseman, Blaine. *Ultimate Fighting: Sporting Championships.* New York: Weigl Publishers, 2011.

Websites

GSP Official Site   http://www.gspofficial.com
The official site for Canadian legend Georges St-Pierre is complete with photos, videos, news, and an upcoming schedule. The site also includes a link to a GSP's anti-bullying foundation.

Jon Bones Jones Official Site   http://www.jonnybones.com
The official site for the youngest UFC champion in history is rich in photos, news, and lots of videos.

Sherdog   http://www.sherdog.com
Calling itself the global authority on mixed martial arts, this site has it all, including fighter rankings, news stories, video content, a fighter database, and much more.

Ultimate Fighting Championship   http://www.ufc.com
The official site for the UFC features fighter biographies, title history, information on upcoming fights, and the informative *New to UFC* section with a glossary, rules, and other introductory information.

***USA Today*—UFC**   http://www.usatoday.com/sports/ufc
The national newspaper leads the way in MMA coverage, with articles and photos.

Yahoo Sports!   http://sports.yahoo.com/ufc/
This site is the place to be before any big fight. Check out the analysis from MMA experts, as well as links to results from past fights.

INDEX

ABOUT THE AUTHOR

Patrick Jones has been at times in his career a librarian, a consultant, a trainer, and a novelist. Through it all, he has always been a fight fan—following both mixed martial arts and professional wrestling. Jones can be found outside of the octagon at www.connectingya.com.

Photo Acknowledgments

The images in this book are used with the permission of: AP Photo, pp. 4, 12; © The Bridgeman Art Library/Getty Images, p. 6; © Warner Brothers/Getty Images, p. 9; © Evan Hurd/Sygma/CORBIS, pp. 10, 15; Cannon Films/courtesy Everett Collection, p. 13; AP Photo/Laura Rauch, p. 16; © Jon Kopaloff/FilmMagic/Getty Images, p. 18; © Gary A. Vasquez/USA TODAY Sports, pp. 21 (top), 23, 38; © Mark J. Rebilas/USA TODAY Sports, p. 21 (bottom); © Mitchell Layton/Getty Images, p. 22; © Jayne Kamin-Oncea/USA TODAY Sports, p. 24; © Mark Kolbe/Getty Images, p. 25; © Holly Stein/Getty Images, p. 27; © Brian Bahr/Stringer/Getty Images, p. 28; © J. Kopaloff/Getty Images, p. 29; AP Photo/Jeff Chiu, pp. 31, 35; © Niall Carson/PA Photos/Landov, p. 37; © Barry Sweet/Landov, p. 39; AP Photo/Kamil Krzaczynski, p. 41; © Scott Cunningham/Getty Images, p. 42; AP Photo/Eric Jamison, pp. 43, 47 (top); AP Photo/Isaac Brekken, p. 44 (top); AP Photo/FEG/Dynamite USA II/Bob Riha, Jr, p. 44 (bottom); AP Photo/Jane Kalinowsky, p. 45; © Barry Sweet/ZUMA Press, p. 46; AP Photo/The Canadian Press/Nathan Denette, p. 47 (bottom); © Tom Szczerbowski/USA TODAY Sports, p. 48; Jorge Cruz/Landov, p. 49; © John Gichigi/Getty Images, p. 51; AP Photo/The Canadian Press/Chris Young, p. 55; Igor Kralj/PA Photos/Landov, p. 57; Paulo Whitaker/REUTERS/Newscom, p. 58 (top); AP Photo/Jae C. Hong, p. 58 (bottom).

Front cover: © Scott Cunningham/Getty Images/Getty Images. Jacket flap: © Mark Kolbe/Getty Images (top); AP Photo/Laura Rauch (bottom).

Main body text set in Adobe Garamond Pro Regular 14/19.
Typeface provided by Adobe Systems.